Since I was in elementary school, I think the word "lunch box" has been associated with sandwiches packaged in bags and snacks individually packaged in cloth lunch boxes. However, insulated lunches will revolutionize lunchtime, making it easier than ever to enjoy meals on the go and comfortably carry them. Using office and kitchen microwaves can be an unpleasant experience. Almost every office has an employee who insists on heating the fish in a communal microwave. Worse still, they arrived late to the shared kitchen and stood by the microwave, trying to "eat it all up" most of their lunch break. Insulated lunchboxes have the added benefit of eliminating frustrations anytime, anywhere, and no longer tasting co-workers' salmon.

WAYS TO DECORATE YOUR BENTO BOX

I have to admit that sometimes it's a hassle to prepare my lunch. And I don't even have to do it every day. I often lack ideas, time, and will. The truth is, I'm almost a lack of enthusiasm. However, I recently noticed that changing the way lunch is presented avoids habits and makes me feel better. It's a three-word solution: color, shape and accessories.

So, here are three ways to decorate your lunch!

Diversified accessories

To complete your lunch box, you can buy accessories to add to your lunch box, such as cute storage bottles, colorful silicon containers for food, cheese, vegetables, and small knobs for chewing ham. ..

Personalize your lunch with Bento Art Accessories and have fun! Use for cherry tomatoes, cheese, vegetables

Diversify your colors

This is the simplest and easiest suggestion on this list. It is often said that to have a healthy diet, you have to change the color of the food. Well, this also helps to make a more attractive lunch! Simple examples: Cherry tomatoes and small carrots in orange-red shades, eggs in yellow, salads in green, rice in white ... it's very easy to add.

If you need more color, you can add spices such as curry or turmeric to the rice to make it yellow, or you can make a small paprika red. You can find more ideas here and there. You can also use plenty of colorful accessories!

Making a delicious lunch of oranges, greens, whites, reds, oranges and browns is not that difficult.

Diversify your shape

There is no doubt that it will take a little longer than changing the colors, but the results will be even better! You should only use a knife if you are motivated enough, or use a well-shaped hood cutter.

For example, you can choose to cut carrots into flowers, apples into rabbits, and cocktail sausages into octopuses. You can also use a food cutter to cut the sandwich into elephants, giraffes, etc. Finally, there is also an egg shape for cooking eggs into cute shapes.

To make you feel cheerful, you can add cute carrot and cucumber flowers, or for a special person, you can easily cut the heart shape into your lunch box, like the bread and cannelloni here. Your special feelings are loved!

HOW TO MAKE BENTO

Plan Ahead

With a little planning, you'll see how easy it is to prepare a healthy lunch that both you and your kids and family can enjoy five days a week. If you have planned your daily dinner together with your weekly diet plan, you can have a significant percentage of your healthy food free. When planning your lunch, you may find that you only need to prepare an extra portion of your dinner so you can pack leftovers for lunch the next day. Easy!

Bento Can Be Used for Many Cuisines
There are no restrictions on the contents of the lunchbox. Lunch boxes such as sandwiches, wraps, pasta and salads may also be included. Other snack foods such as cheese and crackers may also be included. As mentioned above, you can also fill your lunch with soup or stew with a lunch special.

Start With the Right Container

Lunch box packed lunch box can be stylish or simple as you like. You can choose from different brands and styles of lunch boxes at different prices. However, when choosing a lunch box that is right for you and your lifestyle, keep the following important characteristics in mind of your lunch box.

The box has a tight lid.

The container has a partition. Create two partitions with a minimum of one partition, or create up to three to four partitions. Note: Lunchboxes can also be packed in plain containers, without dividers.

Most bento containers are flat, while other bento styles are cylindrical and have separate compartments that can be stacked for both soup and solid food. If you like soups and stews, this bento style might be the best choice.

Accessorize

The bento and jewelery market is large enough for consumers to choose from traditional Japanese and Asian supermarkets and a wide range of products available online.

The accessories are as follows.

Fork
Spoon
Chopstick
Skewers or small tongs – pick up small food
Decorative Silicone, Paper, or Aluminum Food Cups (or Baking Cups) in Different Shapes and Sizes – For Different Types of Food
Food dividers (small and thin silicone dividers) – used, for example, to separate foods with sauces from fruits

Balance and Aesthetics

Balance:

One of the most important things in packing a lunch box is nutrition. It contains plenty of vegetables and fruits, and a moderate amount of lean protein and whole grains in a small amount of milk.

The following ratios for a balanced diet:

40% vegetables
30% whole grain
20% protein
10% fruit

Aesthetics:
Once you have decided on the items for your lunch, pack them properly and firmly. Try packing vegetables and fruits in one part of the lunch box and grains and proteins in another part of the lunch box.

Use bento accessories (partition plates, skewers, etc.) to separate food and add aesthetics. Keep in mind that the tighter the food is packed in the lunch box and the less space there is, the easier it will be to maintain the aesthetics of the lunch box and the more food will fit in place.

HOW TO DECORATING YOUR BENTO BOX

Bento is a convenient way to pack your lunch at work or school. Assembling a do-it-yourself bento box is very easy. All you need is a food container, rice, toppings and colored fruit. But an important aspect of a great bento box is the decoration! Here are basic instructions on how to assemble and decorate a lunch box.

Perfect to put in Studio Ghibli lunch boxes, snacks and lunch boxes!

Necessary things:

Lunch box: You will need a lunch box or food container to start assembling your lunch box. From plain plastic Tupperware to handcrafted lacquerware, there are many options to choose from.

Vegetable and Fruit Shapers: Not only can you chop vegetables and fruits, but you can also take them to the next level by cutting them into beautiful shapes like flowers, hearts and stars. You can find different shapers online. All you need to do is cut vegetables and fruits into round pieces, then press them with a shaper. For vegetables that are difficult to cut, you can boil them in water for a few minutes to soften.

Egg Shape: Egg molds are a cute way to spice up an ordinary hard-boiled egg. To make eggs, first take small and medium eggs and boil them in water. When the eggs are cooked, take them out and wash them with cold water and scrape off the shells. Egg molds are most often used while the eggs are warm because they are more flexible and easier to shape. Soak a peeled egg in hot water for a few seconds to warm a cold egg. After heating, put the eggs in the egg press and keep in place for 10 minutes.

Sauce container: You need to prepare a sauce container so that you can store the sauce separately from the food. This prevents the sauce from mixing with the food unintentionally and prevents the food from sticking.

Organize: Once you've prepared the box, you'll need a silicone cup and dividers, and a food tong to keep your food organized and separate. Silicone cups are a good way to keep food separate, as well as keep dry and wet foods separate.

Partitions are used to separate food and separate portions. You can use plastic dividers and edible dividers like salad leaves. Choose foods that come in cute colors and patterns to help you add fun and color to your lunchbox, or organize loose foods like meatballs and berries.

A rough guide to decorating a nice lunch box is to make sure it's colorful. This means getting lots of colorful fruits and vegetables to bring the box to life. You also need to add interest and depth to your box by incorporating fun shapes and designs. Here are some fun ideas to add some fun to your lunch box decor.

Colored Rice: Rice usually makes up the bulk of a lunch box, as rice is the main carbohydrate in the diet. Not only can you put rice in the box, but you can also add a fun design to the rice, such as mixing it with a sprinkle. You can also color the rice by mixing ingredients like salmon paste, curry powder, and grated carrots.

Bento Cutter: If you want to take your lunch box to the next level and add fun designs or faces to your dishes, you can decorate it with seaweed. Cut the desired shape from a sheet of dried seaweed and place it on top of the food. If you find it difficult to cut out individual shapes, you can use a bento cutter to cut out shapes that suit your design and arrange to your liking.

Decorating your lunch definitely takes more time than wrapping a simple sandwich in your lunch. However, if you have a lunchbox for a loved one or for yourself, you should try a little harder to make your lunch more enjoyable. We hope that this important guide to decorating your lunch box will give you inspiration to make your own.

CONTENTS

Ways to decorate your bento box 10

How to Make Bento 16

how To Decorating Your Bento Box 25

AVOCADO SHRIMP SALAD 39

Stuffed Bagel Sandwiches 41

GREEK YOGURT CHICKEN SALAD 43

Tuna Protein Bento 45

Creamy Pasta Salad with Broccoli and Raisins 47

Spicy Chicken Meal 49

HONEY LEMON CHICKEN 52

Egg mayo, ham and watercress sandwich 55

Prawn summer rolls 57

TUNA SALAD 64

Taco Salad Bento Box 66

Garlic Ginger Chicken & Broccoli 68

Slow Cook Meal Burrito 71

Chicken and sweet potato shawarma 74

Vegan Macadamia Coconut Tofu 78

Dukkah Roasted Vegetables Salad 82

Grilled Veggie & Black Bean 86

- **BREAKFAST TACO BOWLS** 89
- **LOW CARB GREEK CHICKEN** 93
- Mayo-Less Potato Salad 97
- Greek Pita Bento Box 99
- Honey Sesame Chicken with Broccolini 101
- Pasta Salad 108
- Tabbouleh Salad 111
- Super-salad wraps 114
- Healthy Mexican Chicken 116
- Pan Chicken Tinga 120
- Buffalo Chicken Meatballs bento 123
- Greek Healthy Meal 125
- Turkey Meatballs with Zucchini Noodles 132
- Creamy Kale Caesar Salad 135
- Sesame Ginger Zucchini Noodles 137
- Meal Prep Moroccan 140
- Sesame chicken noodles 143
- Falafel lunchbox 145
- Smoked mackerel Caesar salad 147

CHICKPEA SALAD SANDWICH

Material

For Salads:
- 1 (425g) Chickpeas, drained and rinsed (also known as Garbanzo)
- 1/4 C (55g) + 1Tbs dill dill pickles
- 1/4 C (35g) Minced red onion, about 1/2 onion

- 2 Tbs (30g) Choose mayonnaise or vegetables or mayonnaise
- 2 1/2 teaspoons iced mustard
- 1 1/2 teaspoons apple cider vinegar
- 1/4 + 1/8 teaspoon sea salt
- 2 teaspoons chopped fresh dill
- Optional 1/8tsp ground turmeric for color and health!
- Grind 8-10 fresh black pepper

For the sandwich (optional):
- Multigrain bread or optional gluten-free bread
- Germination
- Kale
- Shredded carrot
- lettuce
- tomato

Guide

Use a potato masher to mash the chickpeas until most of them are crushed, but the whole chickpeas are still there. Add pickles, onion, mayonnaise, mustard, vinegar, salt, cumin, turmeric, and pepper to taste. Mix. Seasoning adjusters.

Store in a covered container for up to 2 days. Delicious alone or layered on top of seeds with veggies.

AVOCADO SHRIMP SALAD

Element

- 1/2 tablespoon of olive oil (or if you have avocado oil)
- 2 lemons (lemon juice)
- 1/4 small purple onion
- 1/4 teaspoon salt
- 1/4 teaspoon pepper

- 1/8 teaspoon celery salt
- 1/2 cucumber, pomegranate seeds
- 1 pound of cooked shrimp, peeled, sowed and sowed
- 1/4 cup fresh tomatoes, pomegranate seeds
- 1 avocado, pomegranate seed
- 1 tablespoon coriander

Guide

In a small bowl, add purple, juice, olive oil, celery salt, salt and pepper. Marinated the onions for 5-10 minutes.

Then mix the chopped shrimp, avocado, tomatoes, cucumbers and coriander well and then slowly. Sprinkle over the mixture and gently add again for a uniform coating.

Place in the refrigerator for at least 30 minutes. For all UNES this is a development priority

STUFFED BAGEL SANDWICHES

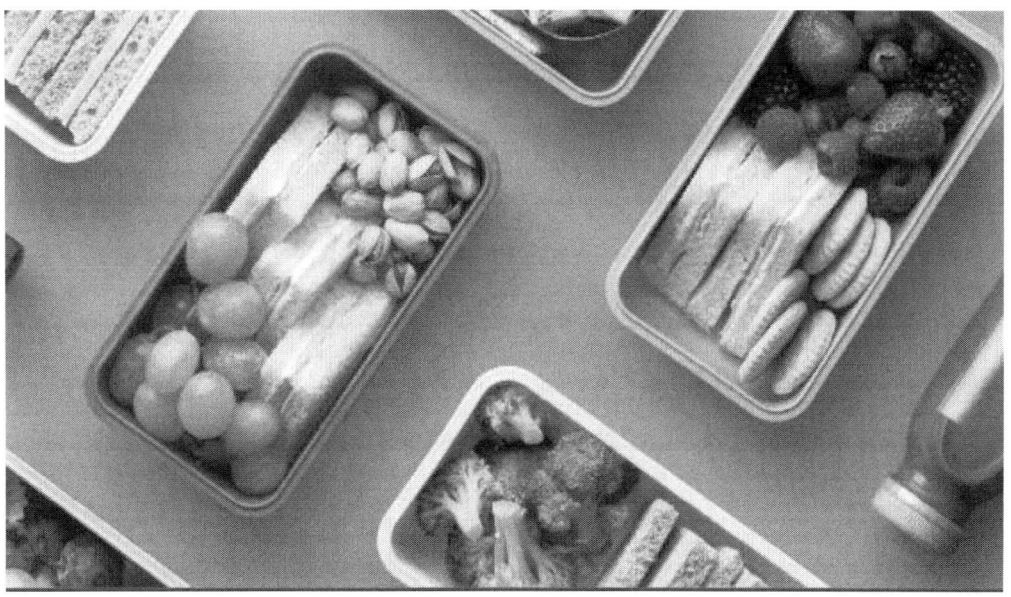

Material

- 1 large bagel or 2 small bagels
- 1/4 cup whipped cream cheese
- 2TB is Relish
- Two large slices of Italian sausage, diced
- 4 carrots, diced
- A pinch of salt and pepper (pinch = about 1/8 teaspoon)

- (A little garlic powder is great for your garlic lovers too!)

Procedure

Cut the bagel from the center and remove most of the excess bread crumbs inside to form a ring. Cut the bagels in half and cut out some sections.

Then add the rest of the ingredients in a mixing bowl until well combined. I usually use a stand mixer for this

Pour cream cheese mixture into the empty bagel half ring.
Spread cream cheese on half of the bagel
Place the other half on top and cut in half.

GREEK YOGURT CHICKEN SALAD

Material

- 2 cups of chopped chicken
- 1/4 cup diced celery
- 1/4 cup raisins
- 1/4 cup plain Greek yogurt I use fat-free
- I love what I did with 1TB SP mayonnaise olive oil
- 1/4 teaspoon salt
- 1/4 teaspoon pepper

Guide

Mix all ingredients in a large bowl.

Allow to cool for at least 30 minutes until all flavors are blended.

Serve with leather, bread, salad and crackers.

Get a delicious Greek chicken salad with just 99 calories with fat-free yogurt and olive oil mayonnaise!

TUNA PROTEIN BENTO

Element

- 4 eggs
- Peel and chop 4 carrots
- Chopped 2-3 celery ribs
- 1 cup of grapes
- 1 cup of blueberries
- 8 ounces of cheese cube

Tuna salad
- 5 ounce can of drained tuna
- 2 tablespoons mayonnaise
- 2 tablespoons of finely chopped celery
- Taste salt and pepper

Guide

Cook and chill hard-boiled eggs (I used an instant pot). Once completely cooled, you can leave the skin on or peel it off.

Stir the ingredients of the tuna salad together and separate between the cans.
Separate all other ingredients into containers.

Store in the refrigerator for up to 4 days.
Enjoy the cold.

CREAMY PASTA SALAD WITH BROCCOLI AND RAISINS

Element

- 1 small broccoli
- Whole wheat elbow Macroni cooked in 1/2 cup
- ⅓ cup raisins
- 1 green onion, white and green parts, thinly sliced
- ⅔ Sour cream cup

- 1 tbsp and 1 tsp apple cider vinegar
- 1 teaspoon honey
- 1 teaspoon yellow mustard
- 1/2 teaspoon kosher salt

Guide

1. Remove the thick broccoli stalks and discard (or save for another meal). Cut the flowers into bite-sized pieces.

2. In a large bowl, mix broccoli, pasta, raisins and green onions.

3. In a small bowl, mix sour cream, vinegar, honey, mustard and salt. Pour the pasta mixture on top and stir until well mixed. Place in a closed container in the refrigerator and store for up to 5 days.

SPICY CHICKEN MEAL

Material

To prepare a chicken meal:

- 1 cup long white rice (quinoa also works - see note)
- 1 cup of water
- 14 oz fresh salsa (undrained canned tomatoes also work)
- 1/2 teaspoon salt

- 1 teaspoon oil
- About 1 pound chicken breast, cut into 4-6 small pieces
- Various seasonings such as cumin, chili powder, garlic powder, and cayenne pepper (taco seasoning also works)

If you want to add it later:

1 can 14 oz black beans, rinsed, drained
A handful of chopped fresh coriander

Procedure

Cooking: Put rice, water, tomatoes, salt and oil in a pan. Mix. Place chicken on top and sprinkle with your favorite seasoning and salt. Turn the Instant Pot on high pressure for 7-8 minutes. When you're done, use the quick release valve for steam.

Mix: Discard the chicken. Mix the black beans (and maybe a bit of sun sauce) with the rice.

Prepare your own meals: Divide rice and beans into 4-6 meal prep containers. Add chicken to each one. Sprinkle with coriander and drizzle with a spoonful of the sauce.

HONEY LEMON CHICKEN

Element

Lemon Chinese Honey Ingredients:
- 2 tablespoons of olive oil or butter, chia seeds
- 1 lb of fresh asparagus *, cut to taste (cut top)
- 2 broccoli, chopped (small)
- Kosher salt and freshly crushed pepper

- 2 lbs boneless, skinless chicken breast, cut to your liking
- 6 pieces of rice or quinoa
- Optional garnish: toasted sesame seeds, lemon slices / seasonings

Ingredients of Sauce Honey Lemon:
- 1/4 cup of water or water
- 1/4 cup of freshly squeezed juice
- Honey 1/4 cup
- 1 tablespoon cornstarch
- 1 tablespoon soy sauce
- 1 teaspoon toasted sesame oil
- A little fiber
- 2 pieces of garlic, squeezed or chopped

Guide

Make Honey Lemon Honey Chicken:
Heat 1 tablespoon of oil (or butter) in a large frying pan or pan. Add asparagus and broccoli, salt and pepper. Fry for 4-5 minutes, stirring randomly until tender. Transfer the asparagus and broccoli to a clean dish and reheat the pan.

Add the remaining one lubricant (or butter) to the pan with the chicken. Season the chicken with salt and pepper. Randomly fry for about 5-6 minutes until the chicken is completely cooked and the pink color disappears. Add the passion fruit sauce over the chicken and simmer for 1 minute or until the water becomes hot and thick. Remove the pot from the heat.

Divide rice, vegetables and chicken evenly into 6 food containers. Top with your desired outfit. Then serve immediately or cover and refrigerate for up to 4 days.

How to make honey lemon sauce:
Evaluate all ingredients together in a set of small dishes or build until combined.

Note

* Let's make a sub with your own vegetables! (Bells, squash, onions, chickpeas, peas, carrots, etc. are all great!)

EGG MAYO, HAM AND WATERCRESS SANDWICH

Element

- 1 egg
- Light mayonnaise 15g
- 1x oat-covered whole grain deli roll
- 1 Slice Wiltshire Healing Ham
- Watercress 10g

Method

Boil the eggs for 9 minutes, drain and cool with running water. Peel and grate in a bowl.

Add mayonnaise and mix well with a fork. Hishaku egg mayonnaise in the lower half of the bread roll.
Place ham and watercress. Upper half sandwich. Wrap in plastic wrap if necessary.

Cooking Tips: As a refreshing snack, you can stuff a cube of cantaloupe melon with peeled, sowed, chopped cucumbers and chopped basil.

PRAWN SUMMER ROLLS

Element

- Chopped lettuce 50g
- Mint 5g, finely chopped
- Grated carrot 30g
- 1 / 2x set of spring rolls
- 5-6 cooked black tiger shrimp, half

Method

Mix lettuce, mint and chopped carrots. Soften half of the spring roll set noodles in boiling water for 5 minutes, then drain.

Soften half of the pancakes one at a time with hot water for 20 seconds. Place shrimp, salad and rice noodles on top of each pancake, roll them up and fold both ends to secure them.

Pack in a lunch box and put half of the kit's tape in another container.

Cook Tip: To add a tropical snack to your spring roll lunch, mix dried mango and fresh coconut with some pumpkin and sunflower seeds and wrap it in a crunch.

CAPRESE CHICKEN SALAD MEAL

Ingredients

- Quinoa - the bottom of this salad provides protein, healthy carbohydrates and nutrients; you'll be able to exchange for the identical amount of farro rice or your favorite grain.

- Tomatoes - I usually don't recommend using tomatoes when preparing food, because they're juicy and tender, but there's nothing wrong with this salad.

- Baby bocconcini - soft mozzarella balls are available at the delicatessen section of your market. Lightweight, soft and saltier than mozzarella pizza

- Fresh basil-basil could be a flavor that covers everything here; Below I share some tips to stay you as young as possible when saving

- Chicken - you'll be able to use chicken breasts, pumpkins or rather than canned peas

Step by step instructions

1. Cook with quinoa- As quinoa cooks and cools for an extended time, start cooking it first. you'll be able to cook quino in many ways:

Fine, fluffy quinoa (hob)
Quick Quinoa Pot
Quinoa cuisine

2. Boil the chicken - Preheat the oven to 425 ° F. Pour 1 kg of lean pigeon breast with 1 vegetable oil and 1 teaspoon balsamic vinegar. Transfer to a baking dish, season with salt and pepper and bake for 25 minutes or until the chicken reaches 165 ° F in an exceedingly very large portion.

When the chicken has rested for a minimum of 10 minutes, cut it against the grain.

Tip - For highly acidic chicken, let it cool completely before cutting (it will retain all the chicken water).

3. Shake the vinaigrette - mix vegetable oil, basil vinegar, syrup and salt and pepper into a smoothie or dressing salad. Divide into food containers.

Tip - If you wish this salad to always be fresh, add dressing before serving.

4. Chambers and storage - Separate cold quinoa, chicken, tomatoes, cherries, mozzarella balls and basil leaves into 4 food preparation containers (2 cups or more). Store within the refrigerator for up to 4 days.

Tip - Keep basil become independent from everything wet and, if possible, add fresh.

5. Serve - When able to serve, garnish with fresh cumin leaves, stir within the salad juice and blend well. give a contribution a salad and enjoy!

Presentation of the recipe
Store fresh basil
Basil is legendary for its fast-growing season, but it gives this salad plenty of flavor and is worth keeping fresh! Here are some ways to try to to it:

Wrap it in towel to stay it fresh.
Keep in a glass with some inches of water, cover the leaves with mulch (out of the sun).

Basil paste is also an option, although we've not tried it yet.

Last place

The salad is stored within the refrigerator for up to 4 days; Expect tomatoes to be moist and tender within 3-4 days. This salad shouldn't freeze.

The difference

Chicken - rather than meatballs, chicken thighs, tofu or soy
quinoa - takes your favorite rice or cereal
balsamic vinaigrette - Switch to at least one of those vinaigrette vinaigrettes or click on a bit of balsamic
Wrap - stop quinoa and wrap it all with tortilla or pita bread

Low Carbohydrate - rather than quinoa cauliflower rice; Change the mint juice and dress it as a sweet fruit, monk

TUNA SALAD

Material:

- Add 2 (5 ounces) of canned tuna to the water, drain and form into flakes.
- 1/2 cup fat-free Greek yogurt
- 1/4 cup diced celery
- 1/4 cup diced red onion
- 1 tablespoon Dijon mustard
- 1 tablespoon sweet and sour pickle, optional

- Taste with at least 1 teaspoon of fresh lemon juice
- 1/4 teaspoon garlic powder
- Taste with kosher salt and freshly ground black pepper
- 2 large eggs
- 4 cards of Vibretas
- 1/2 cup raw almonds
- 1 cucumber, cut into pieces
- 1 Braeburn apple, sliced

Direction:

In a medium bowl, mix tuna, greek yogurt, celery, onion, dijon, lemon juice, lime juice, and garlic powder. Adjust to taste with salt and pepper.

Place eggs in a large saucepan and cover with 1 inch cold water. Bring to a boil and cook for 1 minute. Cover the eggs and remove from the heat. Set aside for 8-10 minutes. Drain, let cool, then peel and halve.

Place the lettuce leaves in the food processor. Add the tuna, eggs, almonds, cucumber, and apple mixture.

TACO SALAD BENTO BOX

Ingredients

- 1 cup black beans
- 1 cup corn kernels
- 3 cups romaine lettuce Wash and withdraw pieces
- ½ Grate cup of cheese
- 1 Cup of dressing of your choice (we recommend dressing coriander, see note!)

- cornflakes
- Pico de Gallo
- Roman tomatoes, sliced
- 1 sliced jalapeno seeds and finely chopped
- 2 tablespoons Spanish onion finely chopped soup
- ⅛ teaspoon salt
- Add 1 lemon teaspoon juice

Suggestions

Divide the components into four storage bins. Use spices before serving to form a separate dressing.

Mix the ingredients for the pico de gallo and boost the jars (make sure the pico doesn't touch the Roman bones).
Store within the refrigerator for up to 4 days. you will want to bring another bowl to serve the salad.

Tip:
We recommend dressing this with coriander and lime
Nutrition information includes dressing

GARLIC GINGER CHICKEN & BROCCOLI

Component

For garlic garlic soup:
- Soy sauce but 3/4 cup
- Water ࿐ 1/2 cup
- 1/4 cup white vinegar
- 1/4 cup oil (lard)
- 2 Inch Fresh Ginger (Peeled)
- 4 cloves of garlic

- 4 days Medjool (you also can use 1/4 cup honey or sugar)

Fly and broccoli:

- 1 pound of boneless chicken or thigh breast, turn over strips
- 1 onion remove inflorescences (about 5 cups)
- 1 red pepper turn over strips
- Sesame oil, sesame seeds and / or green onions to be used

Tips

Preparation sauce: Preheat oven to 425 degrees. Mix all the ingredients well.

Template action: Put chicken, broccoli and red pepper during a pan. Put about 1/2 cup of the sauce on the chicken and just some tablespoons of the vegetable stock. Bake for 10-15 minutes.

Finish it shaped: While the broccoli and chicken are roasting, soak another 1/2 cup or more in a very small saucepan over medium-low heat until it thickens. Drizzle it over the finished chicken and broccoli. Finish with oil, oil or onion. Wow! Enjoy bowling and preparing lunch.

Factor

Sauce: you'll not use all the sauces (I usually have almost half a cup left), but I prefer the additional sauces. Save your remaining soda because you'll be able to just make a fast and straightforward batch of it again next time!

Storage: Refrigerate 3-4 days.

Vegetarian: Sub tofu for vegetarian options! It works well with fries too because the tofu are going to be delicious and caramelized.

Broccoli Structure: a number of the chicken sauce may pass alongside the broccoli during cooking. It makes the broccoli tastier. on behalf of me it doesn't matter because the sauce makes the broccoli very tasty. But if you wish dry and crunchy broccoli, just put it on a separate pan.

Rice or no rice: you'll serve it over delicious rice. But honestly, after I know myself as a food preparation, I don't even miss Hunter! So after all you'll escape without it.

SLOW COOK MEAL BURRITO

Slow burritos

- 1 pound pork shoulder to bone
- Kosher salt and freshly ground black pepper
- 2 tablespoons oil
- ¼ Beef bowl
- Smooth deposit 1
- 2 juice deposits

Deposit 1 can of green chillies 4 ounces
- 2 tablespoons onion
- Coriander 1 tablespoon
- 1 teaspoon garlic powder

Side
- 1 1 cup Greek yogurt
- Deposit 3 lemons
- ½ teaspoon of taco condiment
- 1 liter of cherry tomatoes, half or quarter
- ccහා Spanish onion, onion
- Kosher salt and freshly ground black pepper
- 14 ounces of canned beans, canned and rinsed
- Deposit 2 avocados, sliced
- 1 novel
- ½ Cups of coriander leaves
- Spicy Fresno 1 head, thinly sliced

Suggestions

1. Prepare the minced meat: Boil the minced meat with salt and pepper. in an exceedingly very large skillet, heat the water over medium heat. Add the pork and sear until well browned on all sides, 8 to 10 minutes.

Transfer the pork to a slow cooker. Add stock, vinegar, lime juice, sweet pepper, coriander, cumin and garlic powder. Open the slow cooker and cook until the meat is tender, about 7 hours. Chop the pork with a fork.

3. Prepare the sides: in an exceedingly small bowl, mix the Greek yogurt, half a juice and condiment.

4. during a medium bowl, mix the tomatoes, Spanish onion and lime juice; Season with salt and pepper.

For the filling, divide the grated pork between the four barrels, adding some quarter of each. Next to the meat, make a row of tomato mixture, then a row of black beans, then a row of avocado slices and eventually, a row of Romanian lettuce.

Garnish with coriander, sliced, pepper and also the rest of the lime, remove strips. Wet the yogurt mixture before serving.

Serve immediately or refrigerate for four days.

CHICKEN AND SWEET POTATO SHAWARMA

Ingredients

- 2 pounds of boneless pigeon breast, take away bite-sized pieces
- 1 tablespoon honey
- 2 teaspoons peppers
- 2 teaspoons of cumin

- 2 teaspoons kosher salt and pepper
- 2 juice sediments
- Garlic cloves, chopped or mashed
- pinch of crushed red pepper flakes
- 5 tablespoons vegetable oil
- 2 potatoes, sliced into matches
- 1 bundle of asparagus, ends sliced
- 4 cups boiled couscous or quinoa
- 1/2 cup cashew nuts and dried tomato oil, remove the oil.
- Goat cheese, salad, avocado, sliced cucumber, pickled Spanish onion, pineapple, lemon, mint and coriander, to serve
- Garlic tahini yogurt
- 1 cup plain Greek yogurt
- Tahini 2 tablespoons soup
- 1-2 cloves of garlic, chopped or mashed
- A deposit of 1/2 juice
- Add 1 tablespoon of fresh spicy soup

Suggestions

1. during a large bag, mix chicken, honey, pepper, pepper, salt, pepper, juice, garlic, red pepper and a couple of tablespoons of oil and blend well. Close and refrigerate for half-hour or up to 12 hours.

2. Preheat oven to 425 degrees F.

3. Place the sweet potatoes on an outsized plate and leave with 2 tablespoons of vegetable oil, salt and pepper. Transfer to the oven and bake for 15-20 minutes, then turn and bake for an additional 15-20 minutes.

4. Place the asparagus on a baking sheet and leave with 1 tablespoon of oil, salt and pepper. Transfer to the oven and bake for 10-15 minutes.

5. Place the cooked chicken on an oversized baking sheet and spread in layers. Transfer to the oven and bake for 15-20 minutes, or until chicken is baked.

Divide the ferns into 4-6 jars and arrange chicken, potatoes, bamboo shoots, lentils, lentils and sun-dried tomatoes. Alternatively, couscous, chicken and vegetables are often stored in separate containers and assembled when ready. Food are going to be stored within the refrigerator for up to 1 week.

7. Before serving, heat each bowl if desired and add garlic yogurt (see below) and therefore the necessary icing.

Garlic tahini yogurt
1. Mix all the ingredients during a small bowl. Taste and fits taste. Store within the refrigerator for up to 1 week.

VEGAN MACADAMIA COCONUT TOFU

Element

For brown rice:
- 1 cup of short brown rice
- 2 cups of water
- A little salt
- For tofu:
- Nasoya Extra Farm Tofu 1 pack

- 2 tablespoons of coconut powder
- 1/2 teaspoon salt
- 1/2 teaspoon dill
- 1/4 teaspoon cayenne pepper
- 2 tablespoons of coconut oil

For sweet potato coconut milk mix
- 1 (15) ounces of coconut milk
- 1 large sweet potato, diced inch
- Cut 1 red pepper into large cubes
- 1/2 teaspoon turmeric powder
- 1/2 teaspoon salt
- Freshly ground black pepper
- To assemble:
- 1 package (5 ounces) baby spinach
- 1/4 cup macadamia nuts, chopped
- Chopped fresh coriander

Guide

Cook rice: Put water and brown rice in a medium pot with a small amount of salt and heat over high heat. Bring the water to a boil, reduce the heat to low, cover and cook for about 35-45 minutes until the water is absorbed. The rice is cooked and is a little chewy. Tap with a fork to remove from heat.

To cook tofu: Wrap a few paper towels around hard tofu and squeeze lightly to release excess liquid. I wanted to dry it as much as possible so that it wouldn't crumble.

Next, cut the tofu into 1 inch squares. Place in a large bowl and add coconut flour, salt, cumin and cayenne pepper. Gently throw and mix.

Place coconut oil in a large non-stick pan and heat over medium heat. When the oil is hot, add tofu and simmer on both sides for 3-4 minutes until light brown. When you're done, transfer it to disk for later use.

To cook sweet potatoes: In the same pan, add coconut milk, sweet potatoes, red pepper, turmeric and salt. Bring to a boil, add sweet potatoes, and simmer for 10 to 15 minutes until the fork is tender. Coconut milk needs to be adjusted properly.

Add brown rice ¼, sweet potato / coconut milk mixture (can be mixed with rice if desired), tofu ¼, and a handful of spinach to assemble a bowl. Place macadamia nuts and coriander.

Serve immediately or store in a food preparation container for lunch / supper throughout the week.

DUKKAH ROASTED VEGETABLES SALAD

Material

- 5 cups chopped cauliflower
- 2 cups sliced or minced white button mushrooms
- 1 cup sliced peeled onion or 1 purple onion
- 1 cup grape tomatoes (halved)
- 1/4 c olive oil or butter (add as needed)

- 1 tablespoon duqa or more (see DIY combination note)
- 1 teaspoon minced garlic or 1/2 teaspoon garlic powder
- 1 cup chopped mixed greens (spinach, kale, or Brussels sprouts)
- 1/4 c raw pumpkin seeds (pumpkin)
- Pinch of black pepper
- Sea salt knob
- 2 teaspoons lemon juice
- 2 mint leaves (chopped, garnish) - optional
- A sprig of oregano, garnish
- Garnish with sliced lemon
- Garnish with greens or bean sprouts
- Grated feta or optional parmesan cheese (omit pareo/vegan)
- Garnish with optional dried fruit.
- Optional cream sauce

Guide

Preheat oven to 425F. Spread parchment or grease on a large skillet. Save it.

In a large bowl, add all the cauliflower, mushrooms, tomatoes and diced/chopped onions.

Add 1/4 cup of oil, then add the Duqqa seasoning mix, garlic, salt and pepper and add again.

Mix the chopped greens and stir again. If you want to make your salad more bulky, add vegetables.
Arrange the chopped vegetables on the top plate and sprinkle the pumpkin seeds on top.

Season with salt, pepper and fresh lime juice.
Bake in the oven for 15-20 minutes and check for perfection for 15 minutes.

When the cauliflower is golden brown, take it out of the oven and put it in the pot.
Serve with a few fresh mint leaves (optional), lemon slices, and a few fresh oregano leaves.

Arrange on a plate with extra greens or sprouts. You can simply put it in a large serving bowl.

Sprinkle with excess olive oil if necessary. Or use your favorite creamy makeup. I like to use hot onion sauce.

If you want this salad to be more filling, add a few tablespoons of chopped dried fruit and crushed feta cheese.

Note

If you don't have Duqqa seasoning, you can easily make your own. Replace 1 tablespoon of Duqa seasoning with:
- 1 teaspoon of dill
- 1 teaspoon sesame seeds
- 1/2 teaspoon coriander seeds
- 1/4 teaspoon sea salt/pepper each
- 1 teaspoon toast or finely ground hazelnuts
- A pinch of sugar, red pepper, and cumin seeds, optional.

This grilled salad is great on its own, or you can add cooked cereal, dried fruit, feta cheese, lentils, chicken or beef for free.

Estimated nutrition per serving depends on the Duqqa blend used and does not include sauces or feta cheese.

GRILLED VEGGIE & BLACK BEAN

Element

BBQ Viniglet
- 2 tablespoons of white wine vinegar
- 3 tbsp barbecue sauce
- 2 glasses of honey
- 1 teaspoon lime
- 1/4 teaspoon chili powder
- 1/4 teaspoon salt

Meal preparation bowl
- ¾ Cup raw quinoa
- 1 tablespoon of olive oil
- Salt and pepper
- 1 zucchini, chopped
- 2 chopped peppers
- Chopped purple onions ½
- Drained 19 ounces of black beans and rinsed

Guide

Shake all the vinegar ingredients together and set aside.

Cook and cool the quinoa according to the instructions on the package.
Put the barbecue on medium to high heat.

Mix vegetables, olive oil and salt and pepper in a large bowl. Place on a roasting pan, turn over every 5 minutes and bake for 10 to 15 minutes.

Divide into 4 2 cup containers of quinoa, grilled vegetables and black beans.

Sprinkle with vinegar oil.
Store in the refrigerator for up to 4 days and refrigerate.

BREAKFAST TACO BOWLS

For potatoes

- 1.5 pounds small yellow potatoes, also known as "2-byte potatoes", half
- 2 tablespoons extra virgin olive oil
- 1 teaspoon adobo seasoning (I use Frontier CO-OP)
- Kosher salt, flavor
- Pepper, flavor
- For meat

- 1 tablespoon olive oil
- 1 pound minced beef
- 1/4 teaspoon dill
- 1 teaspoon chili powder
- 1/4 teaspoon garlic powder
- Kosher salt, flavor
- Pepper, flavor
- 1 teaspoon tomato paste
- 1/4 cup chicken soup

For eggs

- 8 eggs
- 1 tablespoon
- Kosher salt, flavor
- Pepper, flavor
- For service
- Chopped coriander
- Picodegallo or salsa
- Cut into lemon and season
- procedure
- Preheat oven to 375 degrees.
- Spread the potatoes evenly on the top plate.

Drizzle the potatoes with extra virgin olive oil. Season with adobo, kosher salt, and pepper and toss to coat evenly.

Put the potatoes in the oven. After 15 minutes, remove the potatoes from the oven and toss them. Return to oven and cook 15 minutes more or until golden and tender.

Heat a large skillet with olive oil over medium to high heat. Put minced beef in a frying pan. Start burning the beef and mash it after the spoon.

When the meat is golden brown, add cumin, paprika, garlic powder and salt and pepper to taste.
Continue cooking while crushing with a spatula until the meat is no longer pink in the center (about 5-7 minutes).

When the meat is golden brown, add the ketchup and chicken broth. Stir it and cook for 2 more minutes. Then remove the meat from the stove and set aside to cool.

Eggs to the bowl.
Using a fork or whisk, mix and beat the eggs vigorously until they form a whipping substance.

In a saucepan, melt buttermilk over medium heat. Turn the pan so the butter is evenly distributed on the bottom of the pan.

Pour the beaten eggs into the pan. Reduce immediately to medium/low heat.

Use a spatula to beat the eggs slowly and gently. When the eggs start to set, use a spatula to push the eggs towards the center. Continue pushing the egg towards the center for about 4 minutes until the egg is fully cooked and fluffy.

Finish with kosher salt and pepper.
To serve, combine a portion of potatoes, tacos, and eggs into the Tupperware. Garnish with coriander, picodegallo and lemon.

LOW CARB GREEK CHICKEN

Element

- 1 lb chicken breast (about 3 cups after cooking)
- 1 1/2 teaspoon sea salt (divided, for salt water)
- 3 tablespoons of olive oil (divided into 1 tablespoon and 2 tablespoons)
- 1 tablespoon balsamic vinegar (optional)
- 1/2 teaspoon black pepper (split)

- 10 ounces of zucchini (cut in half thin, 1/4 inch thick, about 2.5 cups)
- 1/2 lb of grape tomato (half, about 1 cup)
- 1/2 large onion (cut in half and up to 3/4 cup)
- 1/2 tablespoon dry dill
- 1/2 tablespoon of dried parsley
- 1 teaspoon dried oregano
- 1 teaspoon garlic powder
- 1/4 cup feta cheese (clam, option-dairy free only, pale or whole 30)

Guide

Tap the time in the guide below to start the kitchen timer while cooking.

Preheat the oven to 400 ° F. Place the foil and grease in a large frying pan.

Fill a large bowl with water. Add 2 tablespoons of sea salt and stir until dissolved. Put the chicken in salt water for 10-20 minutes.

Meanwhile, chop the vegetables (zucchini, grape tomatoes, onions).

In a small bowl, stir the dried dill, parsley, oregano and garlic powder together.

When the chicken is salted, tap it to dry and place it in the area of the sheet pan. Bring them closer to each other, but do not touch them.

Use 1 tablespoon of olive oil to coat both sides of the chicken. Marinated both sides of the chicken with 3/4 teaspoon sea salt and 1/4 teaspoon peppercorn. Use half and sprinkle a mixture of herbs on both sides.

Meanwhile, in a large bowl, add the chopped vegetables and the remaining 2 tablespoons of olive oil. Add the remaining 3/4 teaspoon sea salt, 1/4 teaspoon black pepper and the remaining herbal mixture. mix well. Place them on a baking sheet so that the vegetables are not pressed against the chicken.

If you use the optional balsamic vinegar, sprinkle the chicken and vegetables with vinegar. (You can also mix it with vegetables and sprinkle the rest on the chicken.)

Bake the chicken and vegetables in the oven for about 20 minutes until the vegetables are tender and the chicken is completely cooked. Remove from the oven and let the pot rest for 5 minutes.

Cut the chicken and transfer it to a food preparation container. Pour the remaining vegetables. If you don't like milk, sprinkle with feta cheese.

MAYO-LESS POTATO SALAD

Material

- 2 lbs red potatoes, unpeeled, cut into 2-inch pieces
- 3 large eggs
- Two stalks of celery, diced
- Minced red onion cup
- 2 tablespoons chopped parsley

- Sour cream cup
- 1 teaspoon yellow mustard
- 1 tablespoon red wine vinegar
- 1/2 teaspoon salt
- 1/4 teaspoon chili powder
- Freshly ground black pepper

Order

1. Bring water to a boil in the middle pot over high heat. Add the potatoes and eggs (both shells) and simmer for 15 minutes. If the potatoes are not tender after 15 minutes using a fork, remove the eggs and continue to cook for a few more minutes until the potatoes are done. Drain potatoes and eggs, drizzle with cold water.

2. Place the celery, onion and parsley in a large bowl. In a small bowl, mix sour cream, mustard, red wine vinegar, salt, paprika, and pepper to taste.

3. Cut potatoes into 1/2 inch pieces and place in a large bowl. Peel and diced the eggs and place in a large bowl. Pour in the sour cream mixture and mix well. Use immediately or refrigerate in a covered container for up to 5 days.

GREEK PITA BENTO BOX

Material

- 12 slices of cold chicken
- 1 cup Zajiki
- 12 mini pitas (or 1 full size wedge cut)
- Greek salad
- 1 cup cherry tomatoes
- Chop 2 cups of cucumber and remove the seeds

- Chopped chili
- Dice a cup of purple onions
- 2 tablespoons feta cheese (crushed)
- Olives (to taste)

Guide

Stir all Greek salad ingredients together. Divide lunch into four.
All remaining ingredients will be separated into the lunch box.
Warehouse
Store in the refrigerator for up to 4 days.

Service
Enjoy the cold! It is recommended to toast pita bread before using after the third day.

HONEY SESAME CHICKEN WITH BROCCOLINI

Element

Chicken

- 1 lb chicken thigh with skin
- Kosher salt and freshly ground black pepper
- ⅓ Cup chicken soup

- 3 tablespoons of soy sauce
- 3 tablespoons honey
- 1 tablespoon of sesame oil
- 1 teaspoon grated ginger
- 2 pieces of chopped garlic
- 1 tablespoon of vegetable oil

SIDES

- 2 bundles of broccolini, trimming
- 1 tablespoon of sesame oil
- Kosher salt and freshly ground black pepper
- 1 cauliflower rice recipe
- 2 tablespoons of sesame seeds
- A bunch of sliced green onions.

Guide

1. Make chicken: Preheat the oven to 425 ° F. Season the chicken with salt and pepper. In a medium bowl, mix chicken, soy sauce, honey, sesame oil, ginger and garlic.

2. Heat the oil over medium heat in a large frying pan that is safe in the oven. Put the chicken in a frying pan, peel and marinade for about 5 minutes until golden. Turn the chicken skin over.

3. Pour the soup mixture into a pan and heat on medium to high heat for 2 minutes. Transfer the pan to the oven and cook for 15-17 minutes until the sauce is thick and the chicken is completely cooked.

4. Mask preparation: In a large bowl, mix sesame oil and sesame oil. Adjust the taste with salt and pepper. Place it in a single layer on the baking tray.

5. After cooking the chicken, grill the broccolini for 8-10 minutes until the meat is tender.

6. To assemble a meal preparation (or serving) container, divide the cauliflower rice and broccolini into four containers (or plates). Add sesame seeds and onions to the chicken and sauce.

7. Use immediately or refrigerate for up to 4 days.

JERK CHICKEN AND GINGERED BROCCOLI

Ingredients

- Slice fat low to 1/3 cup
- 1/3 cup fruit crush
- 1/3 cup honey
- 2 tablespoons fresh ginger
- 1 teaspoon jerk spices

- 2 tablespoons vegetable oil
- 1/2 kg chicken bones
- 2 heads of broccoli, remove the roses
- 2 cups frozen
- 4 cups coconut rice
- Palestine
- Put 2 cups of sliced pineapple
- 1 jalapeno, carved
- Fresh coriander 1/4 cup, chopped
- Lemon juice or 1 lemon

Suggestions

1. Preheat the oven to 425 degrees F.

2. In a bowl, mix soy milk, fruit juice, honey, 1 teaspoon ginger, 1 clove of garlic and 1 teaspoon of oil.

3. Stir-fry the chicken on the plate with the spices and therefore the sauerkraut portion. Move the chicken to 1 side of the plate.

Alternatively, mix broccoli and eidam with 1 tablespoon of the remaining ginger and 1 tablespoon of sesame juice. Season with salt and pepper. Transfer to the oven and bake for 15-20 minutes or until the chicken is roasted and therefore the broccoli is slightly warmed.

4. At the identical time, transfer the remaining teriyaki sauce to atiny low saucepan and produce to a extreme temperature. Bake for 3 פו5 minutes or until the sauce thickens slightly.

5. Divide the rice between the last 4-6 cups and place the chicken and vegetables on top. Boil the chicken with teriyaki sauce.

Alternatively, you'll be able to store the rice, chicken and vegetables in separate containers and blend when ready. Food are stored within the refrigerator for up to 1 week.

7. Before eating, warm each plate pro re nata and add pineapple, fish tea and fresh juice or juice.

Palestine
1. Mix all the ingredients in a very bowl. Season with salt.

PASTA SALAD

Element

For vinegar:
- 2 cloves minced garlic
- 1/4 cup freshly squeezed lemon juice
- 2 tablespoons oregano leaves
- 1 tablespoon red wine vinegar
- 2 teaspoons kosher salt
- 2 tablespoons granulated sugar

- 2 teaspoons Dijon mustard
- 1/2 teaspoon freshly ground black pepper
- 6 tablespoons olive oil
- 1/4 medium purple onion, diced (1/2 cup)

For the pasta salad:
- 1 pound dry short pasta like Farfalle, fusilli, penne, and orecchiette
- 1 pint cherry tomatoes (about 10 ounces), 1/4
- Pit Kalamon Olive 1/2 cup, half
- 1/4 cup canned diced pimento
- 1/2 cucumber or just grated, diced (about 1 cup)
- 1/4 cup loosely packed fresh basil leaves
- 4 ounces goat cheese, crushed
- 1/2 cup toasted pine nuts (optional)

Guide

Make vinegar. Combine the garlic, lemon juice, oregano, vinegar, salt, sugar, dijon, and pepper in the same glass jar. Add oil, seal jar and shake until emulsified.

Onion melon. Pour 1/2 cup marinade into a large bowl (save the rest for later). Add the red onion, stir well and set aside.

Cook pasta. Bring a large pot of salted water to a boil over medium to high heat. Add pasta and cook until fully cooked according to package directions. Drain and rinse with cold water to cool. Good drainage.

Spring rolls. Place the drained pasta, tomatoes, olives, herbs, cucumber, and basil in a bowl with the sauce. Toss in jacket. (At this point, you can save the salad for several hours.)

Complete the salad. When ready to serve, add the reserved sauce, goat cheese, and nuts, if using, and mix until well-mixed.

TABBOULEH SALAD

Element

- 1/2 cup bulgur (see recipe note for quinoa and cracked wheat version)
- 1 lemon
- 1-2 bundles of flat leaf parsley, washed and dried
- One large bunch of mint, washed and dried
- 2 onions
- 2 medium tomatoes

- 1/4 cup extra virgin olive oil, split
- 1/2 teaspoon salt
- 1/4 teaspoon five-spice powder (optional)
- 1 cucumber (optional)
- Garnish mint leaves
- 1 small bowl and 1 medium bowl
- Knife and cutting board
- Measuring cup and spoon
- spoon

Guide

Soak the rice in water. Place the bulgur in a small bowl and cover with about 1/2 inch of very hot (freshly boiled) water. Set aside for about 20 minutes to soak until soft and still chewy.

Prepare herbs and vegetables. While the wine is soaked, squeeze the lemon and chop the parsley and mint into small pieces. This amount of burger requires about 1/2 cup of packaged chopped parsley and 1/2 cup of packaged chopped mint.

Slice the green onions into 1/4 cups. Chop medium tomatoes. They correspond to about 1 1/2 cups. Chopped cucumber, about 1/2 cup.

you. When you're done, drain excess water and place in a large bowl. Add 2 tablespoons of olive oil, 1 teaspoon of lemon juice and 1/2 teaspoon of salt. Throw to sow. When the herbs are finished, put them in a bowl with burger, but save half of the diced tomatoes for garnish.

Season and toss. Add 2 tablespoons of olive oil and 1 teaspoon of lemon juice to the bowl. Mix everything, season the taste, and adjust the seasonings as needed.

Current. To serve, decorate the tabbouleh with some reserved tomato and mint twigs. Serve at room temperature with crackers, cucumber slices, fresh bread, or pita chips.

Note Note
To make quinoa taburi, use 1 cup of cooked quinoa instead of bulgur.

To make tabbouleh from cracked wheat, use 1 cup of cooked wheat instead of bulgur.

Tabbouleh is very flexible. Feel free to add more or less material to your liking. The All Spice Ground sounds unusual, but it's a good idea to give it a try. It adds a little warmth and spices.

SUPER-SALAD WRAPS

Material

1 tortilla
2 tablespoons humus
1 lettuce leaf
¼ carrot, finely chopped or grated
4 cucumbers and/or 2 slices of avocado
1 tablespoon fresh tomatoes or chopped tomatoes
Some grated cheddar

Method

step 1
Lay the tortillas flat on the board, spread the mulch one-third from the bottom, and place the lettuce on top. Place the carrots, cucumber, and avocado on top of the lettuce and sprinkle with salsa. Cheese sprinkles.

Step 2
Fold the bottom of the wrapper just above the filling, fold the sides, and then roll the rest. Cut in half or chop as shown. Place it straight in the lunch box, or if it's halved, wrap it in paraffin paper first.

HEALTHY MEXICAN CHICKEN

Element

- Southern Turkey
- 1 teaspoon garlic powder
- 2 teaspoons of chili powder
- 1 teaspoon salt
- 1 teaspoon chili powder
- 12 oz skinless boneless chicken breast 2 or 3 chicken breast, see note

- 2 teaspoons of avocado oil
- 2 glasses of lemon juice
- For sauce
- 1-2 pieces of garlic, peeled and crushed
- 1 Avocado, peeled and diced
- 1 tablespoon of freshly ground black pepper
- 1 tablespoon of fresh lemon juice or lime juice
- 1 tablespoon of white or apple cider vinegar and more
- 1/4 cup fresh parsley
- 1/3 cup fresh coriander
- 1/2 teaspoon onion powder
- 1/2 teaspoon garlic powder
- 1/4 teaspoon chili powder
- 3/4 cup unsweetened almond milk
- 1 teaspoon salt
- service
- 10 hard-boiled eggs of your choice (see blog for recommendations)
- 12 to 15 chili peppers for a snack
- 1/2 cup mixed green

Guide

Cook southwestern chicken
In a small bowl, mix the garlic powder, paprika, salt and paprika. Reserve and save 2 cups of seasoning. Sprinkle the seasoning evenly on both sides of the chicken breast.

Put butter oil in a pan over medium heat. While still hot, gently place the chicken breast in a frying pan and simmer on the first side for about 5-6 minutes or until tender. Turn it over and cook for another 5-6 minutes, or until the internal temperature reaches approximately 161-162°F. Sprinkle with lemon juice. Transfer to a plate and leave for at least 5 minutes.

Make coriander farm sauce
Combine all ingredients with a food processor or blender. Process until very smooth. Adjust the taste and add vinegar, lemon juice or salt to taste. Divide evenly into seasoning cups or small reusable containers.

Assemble the food preparation container

Thinly sliced chicken breast.

Divide the mixed greens evenly into 5 food preparation containers. Divide the sliced chicken evenly into containers and place on the green.

Divide the pepper evenly into containers and place next to the chicken and vegetables. Put 2 eggs in each box and sprinkle with the southwestern seasonings. Serve with coriander butter sauce.

PAN CHICKEN TINGA

Material

Baking tray:
- 1 pound boneless chicken thighs
- 3 sliced chili peppers (I used one color each)
- Add 1 teaspoon salt and pepper to taste.
- 1-2 tablespoons olive oil

Tinga Sauce:
- 1 tablespoon olive oil
- Half of the onions, minced
- 2 cloves minced garlic
- 1 to 2 chipotle peppers with adobo sauce, chopped
- 1 teaspoon dried oregano
- 1 teaspoon dill
- 114 ounces can grind roasted tomatoes over the fire
- 1/2 teaspoon salt

Procedure

Chicken and peppers: Preheat oven to 425 degrees. Use paper towels to pat the chicken dry. Place chicken and pepper on baking tray. Drizzle with olive oil and sprinkle with salt and pepper. Roast for 30 minutes or until chicken is fully cooked.

Sauce: Heat olive oil in a skillet while roasting chicken and pepper. Add onions, garlic, plantain leaves and spices. Fry for about 10 minutes. Add tomatoes and salt. Boil for another 10 minutes. Transfer to a blender and blend until smooth.

Finish: Remove the pan from the oven. Cut the chicken into small pieces. Toss the sauce (some, almost, everything... up to you). Serve chicken and pepper with quinoa, rice, cauliflower rice, beans, tortillas, greens, or alone.

Note

Combine this with other ingredients like black beans and quinoa and you can easily have 4 servings! If you serve it alone or with fewer ingredients, you'll probably get close to 3 servings.

You can have a little extra sauce, that's the reason for the party. This sauce freezes very well! Save it for later or add some to a bowl when warming up for lunch.

BUFFALO CHICKEN MEATBALLS BENTO

Ideas for filling bento boxes:

- Delicious meat rolls
- The sky
- Fresh wood deposits
- Sliced cabbage
- The rest ... like these meatballs!

- Seeds / seeds
- Trail tix
- Deposit dry wood
- Save the nuts
- Spicy deposit
- Vegetable chips
- Sandwiches / wraps

How:

Depending on what quantity space your box has, just choose something slightly different to place within the box. try and have a minimum of fruits, vegetables and protein sources for a balanced lunch.

For foods like apples, peppers and avocados that are brown, just squeeze juice or juice over them. you'll also cut fruits, vegetables and sandwiches into shapes for kids!

It's very easy. after you stop viewing lunch as a one-size-fits-all meal, it is simple to place together something tasty and nutritious!

GREEK HEALTHY MEAL

Element

For Greek seasoned chicken
- 3 medium-sized chicken breasts, no bones, no skin
- 1 tbsp extra virgin olive oil
- 1 teaspoon dried oregano
- 1/2 teaspoon drying time
- 1/2 teaspoon dried basil
- 1/2 teaspoon chopped dried onions
- 1/2 teaspoon garlic powder
- 1 teaspoon salt

In the case of Tzatziki (see below for Whole30 Tzatziki)
- 1/2 of peeled and grated cucumber
- 1 cup full fat Greek yogurt or coconut yogurt for a light treat
- 2 large pieces of chopped garlic
- 2 tablespoons of extra virgin olive oil
- 1 tablespoon white vinegar
- Salt spoon
- 1 teaspoon of freshly chopped dill

In the case of cauliflower tabbouleh
- 1 12 oz bag of thawed cauliflower rice
- Medium cucumber ½, peeled and diced
- 1 cup of diced tomatoes (about 2 romas)
- 1 cup of chopped parsley
- Chopped mint leaves ¼ cup, optional
- Two sliced onions, white and light green parts.
- 1 piece of chopped garlic
- Divide 2 tablespoons of extra virgin olive oil in half
- 1/4 teaspoon finely grated lemon zest
- 2 tablespoons of fresh lemon juice
- 1/4 teaspoon crushed red pepper
- 1 teaspoon of salt and taste

For Greek meal preparation bowls
- 3 tablespoons of hummus or Baba ghanoush, 2-3 tablespoons per bowl (total about 3/4 cup)
- 5 Kalamon Olives Approximately 5 per bowl
- Feta cheese crumbles as needed

Guide

For Greek seasoned chicken
Preheat the oven to 400°F. Put all herbs, spices and salt in a small bowl. Apply olive oil to both sides of the chicken breast and sprinkle with a mixture of herbs.

Bake until the meat thermometer reaches 160°F. For a fairly thick brisket it takes about 25-28 minutes. Do not overcook! Remove from oven and set aside for complete cooling.

In the case of Tzatziki (see below for Whole30 Tzatziki)
Place the grated cucumber (for Tzatziki) on a paper towel and align the edges. Gently squeeze the bunch to remove as much liquid as possible and place it on a sieve or colander while preparing the rest of the material to keep the cucumbers drained.

When the cucumbers are drained, mix all the tzatziki ingredients. Add salt to the taste.

In the case of cauliflower tabbouleh
Mix all ingredients and seasons with salt and taste.

Assemble the bowl
Divide the tabbouleh and tzatziki evenly into food preparation containers, add 2-3 tablespoons of hummus or baba ghanoush to each box, and place about 5 kalamon olives on top.

Note
If necessary, decorate with finely chopped feta cheese, chopped fresh parsley, a small amount of olive oil, or freshly crushed black pepper.

Make Baba ghanoush at home using this recipe.
Make Whole30: See below for Whole30 Tzatziki. Ignore broken feta cheese. Be sure to use Baba ghanoush or Whole30 compliant hummus (such as cauliflower).

Make a pareo: Use the following Whole30 Tzatziki. Ignore broken feta cheese. Use Baba ghanoush or green-friendly hummus.

The recipe brings 5 bowls.
The nutritional value shown is a general guideline and reflects the information in one bowl with the ingredients listed along with the humus. Actual macros may vary slightly depending on the particular brand and the type of ingredients used.

To determine the weight of your serving, follow the instructions to prepare the recipe. Weigh the finished recipe and divide the weight of the finished recipe (not including the weight of the food container) by 5. The result is the weight of one serving.

BUTTERNUT SALAD

Material

Frozen Pumpkin 100g
- Red onion 40g, finely chopped
- 1/2 lemon, juice
- 1 teaspoon sugar
- 1 x 210g tin chickpeas, refrigerator
- Mint 5g, shredded
- 2 teaspoons pumpkin seeds, toast

- Frozen peas 75g
- Goat cheese 40g
- 2 teaspoons extra virgin olive oil
- 3 breads, half

Method

Preheat oven to gas 7, 220 °C, fan 200 °C. Bake a pumpkin in an oiled baking tray for 25 minutes.
Mix onion with lemon juice and sugar. Let it soften for 15 minutes. Add chickpeas, mint, pumpkin seeds, and pumpkin. I will pass it on to my lunch box.

To soak, boil beans for 5 minutes, drain, and let cool. Dot with cheese, olive oil, 1 tablespoon water and seasoning. Put it in a carrying case. Packing bread.

TURKEY MEATBALLS WITH ZUCCHINI NOODLES

Element

Meatball

- Non-stick spray
- 1 tbsp extra virgin olive oil
- 1 chopped purple onion
- 2 pieces of chopped garlic
- Freshly chopped parsley ¼ cup
- 3 tablespoons grated parmesan cheese
- 1 pound of turkey minced meat

- ¾ teaspoon kosher salt
- 1/2 teaspoon of freshly ground black pepper

SIDES

- 3 pounds of zucchini, many seeds
- 1/2 teaspoon kosher salt
- 2 cups of marinara sauce
- Parmesan cheese if needed for garnish

Guide

1. Food boil: Preheat the oven to 375 ° F. Line the baking sheet with aluminum foil and spray with a non-stick spray.

2. Heat olive oil over medium heat. Add onions and fry for about 5 minutes until tender. Add garlic and fry for at least 1 minute until fragrant.

3. Transfer the mixture to a medium bowl and let it cool a little. Stir-fried parsley, parmesan cheese and turkey. Adjust the taste with salt and pepper. Shape the mixture into balls (about 2 tablespoons each) and place in the prepared baking tray.

4. Transfer the baking sheet to the oven and bake the meatballs for 17-20 minutes until completely cooked.

5. Make zucchini: While the meatballs are being cooked, put the zucchini and salt in a large colander and leave for 5 minutes.

6. Put salt water in a large pot and bring to a boil. Put the zucchini in water for 1 minute, remove it and drain.

7. To assemble (or serve), divide the zucchini noodles into 4 boxes (or plates). Place meatballs and ½ cup of marinara sauce. Decorate with Parmesan cheese.

8. Use immediately or refrigerate for up to 4 days.

CREAMY KALE CAESAR SALAD

Element

- One big bunch of kale
- ⅓ Cup chopped walnuts, lightly toasted
- ¼ cup sour cream
- Freshly grated parmesan cheese ¼ cup
- 3 tablespoons of extra virgin olive oil

- 1 teaspoon of fresh lemon juice
- 1 piece of chopped garlic
- Salt spoon
- Freshly ground black pepper

INSTRUCTION

Remove the large stems and central veins of the kale, discard them, and cut the leaves into small pieces. Place toasted walnuts in a large bowl.

2. In a small bowl, mix sour cream, palmezan cheese, olive oil, lemon juice, garlic, salt and pepper to taste. Pour the dressing over the kale mixture, cover within 24 hours, and serve.

SESAME GINGER ZUCCHINI NOODLES

Material

- See cup of low salt soy sauce Notes 1
- See 1 tablespoon Master Note 2 fruit sweetener
- 2 tablespoons apple cider vinegar
- See Note 3 for 1 pound of ground beef
- 2 tablespoons sesame oil
- 1 teaspoon finely ground ginger
- 3 cloves of minced garlic
- Two medium spiral zucchini

Guide

Prepare the sauce - with a simple sauce of low-sodium soy sauce, apple cider vinegar, monk fruit sweetener (or honey). Save it.

Cook beef in a non-stick pan over medium heat. Add beef and cook with a spatula for 7-10 minutes or until fully cooked. Carefully drain the pot if necessary.

Add seasoning and sauce to the beef and add sesame oil, ginger and garlic. Cook for 1 minute. Add the sauce, stir and coat the beef. Cook for 1 minute until coating is even and remove from heat.

Part-Use a zucchini spiral to divide the beef into 4 2-cup containers. If using a single compartment, layer the zucchini noodles on top of the beef so it doesn't stick.

Tip:

1-Low Sodium Soy Sauce can be substituted with Bragg's Liquid Amino, Coconut Amino, or Tamari Soy Sauce

2-If low in carbs, you can replace the monk fruit candies with 2 tablespoons of maple syrup/honey

3-Can be exchanged for minced turkey, minced pork, or mashed tofu

Warehouse
Store in an airtight container in the refrigerator for up to 4 days.

Reheat
Heat each portion in the microwave until hot and moist, or cook the entire batch over medium heat for 5-10 minutes in an uncovered pan.

MEAL PREP MOROCCAN

Material

- Cut 2 sweet potatoes
- A cauliflower cut into a flower
- 4 tablespoons extra virgin olive oil
- Kosher salt and pepper
- 2 14 ounces chickpeas, drained and squeezed dry
- 2 garlic bulbs, minced or minced

- 1 inch grated ginger
- 2 cups smoked paprika
- 2 teaspoons dill
- 1 teaspoon chipotle chili powder
- Peel and lemon juice
- A small bunch of coarsely torn kale
- Cook 2 cups of casserole or quinoa
- Carrots, orange part, chopped onion, pistachios
- 1 avocado, cut into pieces

Guide

1. Preheat oven to 425 degrees F.

2. Mix sweet potatoes, cauliflower, and 2 tablespoons olive oil on a large rimmed plate with a pinch of salt and pepper, respectively. Mix well and apply evenly. Transfer to the oven and bake for 20 minutes.

3. In the meantime, pinch in 1 tablespoon olive oil, chickpeas, garlic, ginger, smoked paprika, cumin, paprika, and salt and pepper.

Mix well and apply evenly. Remove the sweet potatoes from the oven and scoop the chickpeas around the vegetables. Transfer to the oven and bake for 10-15 minutes or until chickpeas are crisp.

4. In a medium bowl, massage the kale with the remaining 1 tablespoon of olive oil, lemon juice, and a pinch of salt.

5. To assemble, divide the toasts into bowls. Order grilled vegetables and chickpeas. Add kale, carrots, and oranges. Sprinkle with pomegranate seeds and pistachios. Please keep it in the refrigerator. Add avocado and drizzle with lemon juice before serving.

SESAME CHICKEN NOODLES

Element

- 1 tablespoon tahini
- 1 lemon, juice
- 2 teaspoons of soy sauce
- 2 pieces of grilled garlic
- 1 teaspoon of sesame oil
- 1/2 teaspoon grated pepper and additional serve
- Grilled rice noodles 200g
- Roast chicken leftovers 200g

- 1 Eggplant rang
- 1 grated carrot
- Cucumber ½, sow seeds and cut in half
- 1/2 small packet of mint, chopped

Method

step 1
Put tahini, lime juice, soy sauce, roasted garlic meat, sesame oil and paprika in a large bowl and add enough water to make the sauce.

Step 2
Add the noodles, leftover roast chicken, carrots and carrots and gently mix the cucumbers and mint. Divide into two boxes and sprinkle with a few peppers.

FALAFEL LUNCHBOX

Material

- Cereals or cooked lentils in a 250g bag (use red and white quinoa)
- A handful of young spinach
- ¼ cucumber, chopped
- A handful of cherry tomatoes, half
- 2 grated carrots
- 1 pomegranate, pomegranate seeds

- 10 olives (optional)
- 12 Falafel
- 4 tablespoons humus
- Small olive oil (optional)
- ½ lemon, quarter

Method

Step 1
Divide the seeds between lunch boxes. Put veggies, falafel, a spoonful of hummus, a drop of oil on each,
or keep ingredients separate in a bento compartment.

Just before serving, put lemon in each box and squeeze

SMOKED MACKEREL CAESAR SALAD

Element

- Ciabatta 50g, cut to 1cm. Cube
- 1/2 tablespoon of olive oil
- 1 teaspoon of smoked paprika
- 1/4 teaspoon dried oregano
- 1/2 romaine lettuce heart

- Smoked mackerel 75g, peeled and scales removed
- Shredded parmesan cheese 10g
- Healthy Caesar sauce 40g

Method

Preheat the oven to a gas temperature of 6,200 ° C and a fan of 180 ° C. Mix ciabatta pellets with olive oil, paprika and marjoram. Spread on a small tray and bake for 15 minutes until crispy. Allow to cool before placing in a container.

Divide the romaine lettuce into lunch boxes. Place mackerel and parmesan cheese shavings on top.
Place the Caesar dressing in a pan with a lid. We will provide a mixture of everything.

Chef's Advice: As an optional snack, you can put some berries in a small container.

Printed in Great Britain
by Amazon